NATION OF VICTIMS
The secret in politics and other stories

Michael S. Ericson

Table of Content

Chapter 1

The Nation decline is caused by Victimhood

The current events in Greece serve as a stark warning about what will happen to any country whose population refuse to assume responsibility for their destiny. Greece's excessive spending has resulted to a mountain of debt. The residents' negligence, carelessness, and tax evasion methods have dragged a huge country to her knees, and if something is not done quickly, the end of times may have just arrived for a country that is "anointed" only to borrow!

Roosevelt was the first president to enter the White House in a wheelchair and was most likely the first. Franklin D. Roosevelt served as the 32nd president of the United States of America, which was a record. His unusual election to four terms in office won't likely ever happen again because to the United States Constitution's 22nd Amendment, which was passed shortly after he passed away. Roosevelt made an effect while using a wheelchair even though polio left him paralyzed at the age of 39. You don't need the environment to change for you to have an impact. You can influence where you are and with whom you are if you merely change your attitude and disposition.

Senator Roosevelt was re-elected twice (New York). In 1928, he won the election for governor of New York (the Governor on a wheelchair). The fact that New York's governor uses a wheelchair was not widely known. No one can make you lesser without your agreement, his wife once told him, and that kept him going. You are merely physically disabled; your mind is unaffected. Throughout the Second World War and the Great Depression, Roosevelt presided over America for 12 years. In life, others can halt you momentarily, but only you have the power to do so in the long run.

"You may succeed even if no one else believes in you, but if you don't believe in yourself, you will never succeed." Maxwell

The only limitation in life, according to Hamilton, is a negative attitude. It is sad that extortion in modern-day Nigeria has taken on a disability-related face. The majority of our main roadways and parking lots are occupied by cripples and fake invalids begging for alms. A Yoruba proverb claims that even though beggars will be fed, they will be denied a respectable life.

Because of their victim mentality, the majority of our youths are fleeing the country for the wrong reasons. A liability cannot become an asset simply by changing the context; this is an inherent occurrence. The fact is that leaving the country gives you a stage on which to demonstrate your intrinsic worth, something that is impossible to do in a depressing setting. You have a platform to explore and expand on who you have always been when you travel abroad. Knowing that the majority of Nigerian youths have turned into financial runaways and liabilities on the world stage is sympathetic. This mentality has stifled and severely limited national development. According to Jim Rohn, if you don't create your own life plan, you can end up adhering to someone else's. And do you know what they have in store for you? Not a lot.We must carry out our responsibilities not as victims but as responsible citizens, whether we are in public office, the business sector, or as street cleaners. Our culture of lawlessness and carelessness has severely hampered national development. No matter what field of endeavor they choose, according to Vincent

Lombardi, "the quality of a person's life is in exact proportion to their commitment to greatness."

Either you accomplish great things, or you at least perform little things admirably! Yes, you, I'm talking to you. Stop attributing your anger and failures to the Nigerian system, get past your justifications, get past your upbringing, and decide what it is you were made for—and be prepared to pay a price to be it! Don't use your circumstances as an excuse to avoid taking your proper place in life and eternity. Victims are simple to identify because they are rife with justifications, persistently focus on issues rather than potential answers, and look for faults rather than solutions. You will find a way if your life is that essential to you; if not, you will come up with an explanation. An excuse is worse and worse than a lie since it is a falsehood with guarded truth! Most influential people in life offer little justifications. They are aware that making excuses will not result in action. Living an excuse-filled existence is useless. "I never knew a man who was good at making excuses who was good at anything else," stated Benjamin Franklin.

Either you manufacture excuses or you make progress in life; there are no middle grounds. It is difficult to make excuses in life and still achieve accomplishments. Excuses empower our inadequacies; they do so. By refusing to accept responsibility and finding reasons not to, so many people have essentially deprived themselves of any chance to develop. Going from failure to success is simpler than going from making excuses to success. "Ninety-nine percent of failures originate from people who have a propensity of creating excuses," remarked George Washington Carver. Instead of seeking effective answers to issues, it seems that the Nigerian population is passionate about defending its predicaments. A victim's mindset is a mental disorder, and the cure is as simple as taking responsibility for your life and quitting making excuses for your shortcomings.

In addition, I firmly feel that the Nigerian system needs to be redesigned. Given the clear erosion of our value system, this is now necessary. For the new Nigeria we yearn for, our reward system has become antiquated and out of date. This country's intricate architecture has been created in such a way as to reward those who lack intellectual merit. The Nigerian oil has attracted a large number of bad guys and moral criminals who are using it as an excuse to kidnap, vandalize, and explore for financial gain. The Nigerian system favors intellectuals who find solutions to issues over miscreants and touts who harass. We must rebuild our country such that those who find solutions are rewarded. The reason why there are so many individuals involved in politics is not so they can propose answers to the system, but rather so it can reward political miscreants. When some of our "exalted" governmental office holders are nothing more than glorified drug lords, it is extremely demeaning. a country where politics is a career and professional kidnapping pays better than the work of honorable citizens.

Last but not least, I'd want to talk about parents who have made their kids into victims by pressuring and coercing them to lead lives that they themselves should have led when they were younger. Future planning for a child is outside of the purview of parental "jurisdiction." Instead of giving their kids a platform to blend in with the crowd, parents should resist the urge to mold them into their own image. As a youth coach, I've noticed that the country is creating youngsters who are outwardly docile but internally rebellious—children whose destiny has been violated! children who lack the means to express themselves. Providing a space for their kids to be themselves is the best gift parents can give them. Parents should encourage their children's individuality. The worst kind of parental immorality and abuse is to force our kids to live lives that are not their own.

I've learned from my experience mentoring young people that when expression is restricted, it leads to utter dejection and rebellion. We should encourage our kids to express themselves, be creative, enthusiastic, interested, and inquisitive. The best teachers, in Trenfor's opinion, "show you where to look but don't tell you what to see." I'm encouraging and challenging young people in Nigeria to actively include politics and committed service into their fruitful years. By taking part in the policies and decision-making procedures that will give birth to a new Nigeria, youth should have a beneficial impact. We need to cease abdicating our duties to politicians who only regard the political arena as a retirement home for worn-out intellectual invalids.

Prerequisites for victimization
Another strategy used outlines a number of prerequisites for the emergency tense of feeling like a victim. It implies that people view themselves as
1 Those who believe they were hurt and weren't at fault are considered victims.
2 They were powerless to stop the damage;
3 They are being treated unfairly despite their moral rightness;

4 They merit sympathy.10 The latter requirement expands the definition in important ways. It makes clear that the appearance of the damaging event cannot simply be caused by experiencing it feeling of victimhood This sense requires perception in order to exist. The harm as unjust, unethical, and unwarranted; an act that was unavoidable by the hapless. The requirement for empathy then becomes apparent.

Additionally to the many definitions, the analysis has been elaborated on in a variety of ways victimization has moreover surfaced. As an illustration, it has been suggested that the

The concept of victimhood presupposes that specific individual or group rights were either tangible rights, such the right to food and shelter, or more general rights, are violated. Abstract rights like the right to a happy life, a place to call home, and the right to

identity freedom of expression. Another differential results from this distinction, which.argues that certain victims suffer a real violation of their rights (territory, murder, damage to one's person or), while other victims are impacted by intangible experiences like identity theft, other forms of psychological anguish, and security losseven the loss of one's former self. Victimization is therefore more than just an end in itself.incident, but also on a personal encounter, as some individuals definebthemselves as "victims" in situations that many others would consider to be normal their regular routine.

Additionally, it should be recognized that people might suffer harm both formally and informally. Thus, they may experience psychological or physical harm either do themselves pain or have ties to other victims, and so feel deceived indirectly.Consequently, it is believed that the most The focus should be on the following to help you grasp what it means to feel like a victim:
the experience's negative impact on the person who had it.

One could assert that roles of interactional, procedural, and distributive justice, An individual's psychological state of victimhood is how they view themselves as a victim and/or believes themselves to be a victim, or has "victim beliefs."

The query that should be asked, though, is if the sensation of vi-Timhood is solely based on one's own viewpoint. Many academics add another per-

The analysis should take into account the social context. A "social construction" exists of the victimization notion that designates the traits of a "victim," awards them to the victims and their social setting, and it gives the designation some legitimacy after this

When legitimization occurs, people frequently work to uphold that perception.with time. In keeping with this, it's important to point out that references to victimhood as a social.The meaning of the victim might vary based on culture thanks to building, accordingto various sociopolitical settings

Victimization occurs in the context ofrelationship with a particular area or culture. Because of this, each participant's be In order to understand behavior, one must first understand the relationship and its legal context.

Contexts include the political, social, and economic.19

Foundations

Consequently, the victim complex has three pillars. First, it has a foundation in reality harm that is sustained, either directly or indirectly.

Second, purely individual Perception is insufficient. 'Victim' is also a social title, or, to put it another way, the outcome of social acceptance of an action as causing unlawful injury.

Third, once people understand they frequently make an effort to maintain their status as victims.

Sequential steps:
The victimization process
Thus, victimization can be seen as a dynamic social process that is separated into multiple successive steps that provide a certain person or organization the victim status

For instance, the symbolic interaction theory claims that Victims are defined by the social process as both people and groups.

The experience of a damaging deed, followed by suffering, elimination, and this process attribution of causes for the damaging conduct, self-responsibility for the suffering, and describing the actions and reactions that should be expected.

Some of them view this harm as unjust, unfair, and unwarranted, which to make them believe they are victims;

Some people who believe they are victims try to seek societal acceptance.

gaining approval from others (family, friends, authorities, etc.) believe they are victims and that harm has been done to them;

Some of the people who claim to have been victimized get outside help.

Likewise, suggested five minimal requirements as necessary to qualifyregarding the victim's status:

1. a single damaging occurrence that can be identified;

2. the verdict is unfavorable;

3. the idea that it is an unavoidable event;

4. the identification of a societal or personal offender as the cause;

5. being viewed as going against a social norm.

Based on the aforementioned explanations of the victim's definition and status and conceptualization, we'd want to go on to an examination of the communal perception of victimization, which is the topic of our attention.

Chapter 2

Civil war

A civil war is a bloody battle that takes place on the territory of a state between that state and one or more organized non-state actors. Thus, civil wars are distinguished from interstate conflicts (in which states battle one another), violent conflicts or riots that do not involve states (sometimes referred to as intercommunal conflicts), and state repression of people who cannot be categorized as members of an organized or cohesive group, including genocides, as well as from similar violence by non-state actors, like terrorism or violent crime.

The term "civil war" obviously refers to a wide range of conflicts. Some commentators make a distinction between conflicts when rebels fight for control of the central government and civil wars where they fight for territory independence or autonomy. Conflicts over political power may entail insurgents coming from within the state machinery or the central government, as in military coups, or adversaries from outside the political system. Others make a distinction between revolutionary fights, in which the insurgents seek significant societal change, and ethnic civil wars, in which the rebels and those in charge of the central government have different ethnic identities. Some studies distinguish between colonial warfare and civil wars fought on a state's main landmass. Despite these distinctions, a particular civil war will frequently incorporate a number of them. For instance, insurgencies may have both ethnic and ideological roots, and their objectives may change over time from secession for a specific region to total control of the state.

Armed challenges to state authority date back to the founding of states themselves. There are many historical tales of civil wars, but there is little empirical information on those that occurred before 1945. Civil wars have been frequent since then, despite the fact that there haven't been many interstate conflicts. Civil wars frequently last for a long period, are less likely to be resolved through official agreements, and are significantly more likely to reoccur than interstate battles. The escalation of new civil wars immediately after the end of the Cold War was seen by many experts as evidence that the world would become more turbulent and violent following a protracted period of stability based on the nuclear deterrence strategy adopted by the United States and the Soviet Union. However, after the initial surge following the Cold War, the number of new civil wars actually decreased in terms of relative numbers. The precise reasons for that drop are still up for debate, and the absolute number of active civil conflicts is still substantial.

In terms of the number of people killed in direct combat, civil wars are typically less deadly than interstate conflicts. However, civil conflicts have become more common and prolonged, and during the Cold War, civil wars are to blame for the vast majority of reported deaths in combat. Beyond the immediate cost of life, war can have a significant indirect influence on human welfare. Studies have shown that civil war-torn nations experience a sharp decrease in their gross domestic product and never regain their prior economic development trajectory. A substantial socioeconomic legacy of civil wars includes the unemployment of former combatants and the displacement of civilians. They also impair trade and investment. Civil wars have significant economic effects on neighboring countries as well, and they may make them more violent themselves. Civil wars do not only have negative effects on the countries directly involved.

Civil war's economic root causes

Most civil wars occur in societies that are comparatively less wealthy. Early research on the causes of violence in civilizations tended to emphasize economic hardship and personal grievances. For instance, the American political scientist Ted Gurr highlighted inequality and the potential for revolt among groups who are unsatisfied with their present economic circumstances in comparison to their objectives. The literature on nationalist conflicts placed a strong emphasis on how both relatively wealthy and impoverished groups are prone to rebel against the center if they think they will prosper under independence. Latin American civil wars were frequently seen in the context of economic grievances brought on by either unfair land distribution or significant income disparity. However, there is conflicting empirical support for the link between individual income inequality and civil strife.

Later political-economic analyses of the civil war tended to ignore the significance of complaints. Some researchers asserted that since complaints are commonplace, it is more crucial to concentrate on the variety of opportunities for violence. Paul Collier and Anke Hoeffler, two British economists, claimed that low total income makes it simpler to mobilize insurgencies since potential recruits have less to lose in terms of foregone income from conventional economic activity. According to American political scientists James Fearon and David Laitin, weak states—which are largely influenced by economic development—are the main cause of civil conflict. Researchers in this school have also connected individual incentives to mobilization. When people may profit from battle, such as through stealing or obtaining control of important natural resources, insurgencies have a larger chance of success. The alleged connection between the presence of valuable natural resources and a higher probability of civil war was also substantiated by empirical studies. African civil wars are frequently used to promote those viewpoints.

Another reasonable justification for using violence is political deprivation, such as colonial subjugation or a lack of political rights. After 1945, many conflicts started as movements for independence in colonial-ruled regions. The Indochina Wars (1946–75) and the Algerian War of Independence (1955–1962) inspired movements in other nations by demonstrating how colonial governments that were overwhelmingly more strong might be subdued via protracted violent campaigns. Within empires like the Soviet Union and Ethiopia, numerous ethnically diverse factions engaged in comparable national liberation campaigns.

There is scant proof that ethnic diversity by itself increases a nation's risk of civil war. The degree to which specific ethnic groups are often denied access to political power or subjected to discrimination by the government is more important. If ethnic communities are granted autonomy rights and inclusive institutions, and if access to power or control of the state does not usually result immediately from the relative size of ethnic groups, then ethnically diverse countries are generally not more prone to violence.

Another setting for violence to emerge in authoritarian governments is the fight for expanded political rights. Autocratic regimes often forbid citizens from engaging in political activity and frequently use harsh repression of protests, which might lead people to turn to violence. As in South Africa under the apartheid system, protests against authoritarian or exclusive regimes frequently devolve into violence and occasionally result in protracted conflicts. Even insurgent movements that do not immediately enact democratic institutions once they come to power, claims for increased political rights and freedom are undoubtedly significant components of their rhetoric.

Numerous academics have noted that although authoritarian regimes tend to limit the opportunities for peaceful political expression and protest, they are frequently restrictive enough to stifle any major dissent. Because they combine a lack of political freedom with ample possibilities for protest, which would be lacking under a more repressive regime, regimes that combine autocratic and democratic traits are thus probably the most likely to engage in violent conflict.

Civil war opportunity structures
The majority of the ideas covered above place a focus on structural elements that are either rarely changed or change gradually through time. Such enduring structural characteristics do not offer convincing justifications for why civil wars spring out at particular eras and not at others. According to social movement research, specific occasions might produce "political opportunity structures" that give groups a better chance of winning concessions from the government. Events that facilitate group mobilization—by, for instance,

bringing groups together or identifying focal locations for organizing protests—may include indications of state weakness, disagreement amongst elites, or demonstrations that make it easier for groups to organize. This paradigm can be used to interpret many of the arguments and findings that have already been made in civil war research. Changes in regime and other indicators of a weaker state's power might raise expectations for success or force a government to make concessions. Conflict risk can also escalate as a result of economic and environmental disasters. This is in line with the notion that emergencies and crises can serve as catalysts for mass protests against the government. For instance, a long-running Marxist insurgency saw a sharp rise in recruitment after the 1973 earthquake in Nicaragua, which was followed by significant corruption and a lack of restoration.

Civil war's global implications
Civil conflicts can start and develop as a result of factors that are external to certain nations. The participants in numerous civil wars are not usually limited to the nations where the majority of the fighting occurs. Ethnic groups routinely cross international borders, and relatives from different countries frequently take part in or support uprisings in other countries. For governments and

rebels, the position of international borders generates varied limits and opportunities. Technically, borders are only lines in the sand, and from a strictly military standpoint, they are frequently easy to cross. However, the legal demarcation of state sovereignty by boundaries makes it more challenging for governments to quell insurgencies by rebel groups located in neighboring states. Additionally, the presence of hostilities in a neighboring state might encourage violent mobilization, either through the direct import of weapons and combatants or by the imitation of previous uprisings. And finally, interstate war and civil war are sometimes closely related. Civil wars may encourage military conflict between states, for instance as a result of border violations or claimed backing for insurgents, while poor relations between states may push governments to sponsor insurgencies in competitor countries.

Chapter 3

Theory of Race

The late nineteenth and early twentieth century race theory was founded on flawed reasoning and theories that are now disproven by geneticists. However, they are important looking into since they both help us understand the past of racism and have an impact on how some people still talk about racial disparities now. Race is primarily seen in the twenty-first century as a sociological category that influences how individuals interact with one another (often negatively). The moral, intellectual, or dispositional differences across groups are unaffected by the minute genetic variations between them.

Scientists and anthropologists started discussing the racial disparities between Europeans and the indigenous population in the second part of the nineteenth century. The theory that different races had varied hereditary compositions and, as a result, had diverse physical and mental capacities was being promoted at the time by numerous scientists. They came to the conclusion that some races—typically their own—were superior to others. Soon, academics, politicians, pastors, artists, and others started to denigrate native people and use labels like "redskin" to distinguish them from Europeans.

Samuel George Morton, an anthropologist from the United States, was one of the original proponents of racial science. Morton falsely hypothesized (with very little evidence) that the same is true within the human species; a person's intelligence, personality, and morality, he assumed, were linked to skull size, based on the common observation that humans have bigger brains and more skills than any other animal species. Morton hypothesized that more intelligent groups or races are more advanced than others because they have larger brains, and that this was a "objective" approach to rate the various races he discovered. Morton also thought that a group may be more "civilized" if its cranial capacity was greater. These theories have long been rejected by scientists.

In an 1839 book titled Crania Americana, Morton collected descriptions of each "race" based on his pseudo-scientific classification of humans based on their physical characteristics. Morton contrasts depictions of Europeans, Native Americans, and Africans in the paragraphs that follow.

Europeans
The Caucasian race is distinguished by naturally light skin that can take on any hue and fine, long, curly hair in a variety of colors. The skull is big and oval, with a full and raised anterior region. The face is oval in shape, tiny in relation to the head, and has well-proportioned features. This race is known for its aptitude for achieving the highest intellectual endowments.

Due to its natural fertility, [the Caucasus] has been the breeding ground for numerous nations that have colonized the prettiest areas of the planet and produced some of its most beautiful people.

American Indians
Brown skin tone, long, lanky hair, a lackluster beard, and black hair are characteristics of the American race. The lips are tumid [swollen] and compressed, the eyes are black and deeply set, the brow is low, the cheekbones are high, the nose is big and aquiline, the mouth is wide. The Americans are completely devoid of marine adventure and have a mentality that is hostile to civilization, slow to learn, restless, vindictive, and fond of conflict.

They are cunning, sensual, ungrateful, stubborn, and emotionless, and a large portion of their devotion for their kids can be attributed to entirely selfish goals. They consume the most repulsive [items] raw and unwashed, and they appear to have no thoughts beyond surviving... [Indians] are not only opposed to the constraints of schooling, but for the most part are unable to a sustained process of reasoning on abstract matters... Their mental capabilities, from infancy to old age, present a continued childhood.

Africans
Having a black complexion and black, woolly hair, they also have huge, prominent eyes, a broad, flat nose, thick lips, and a wide mouth. Their heads are long and narrow, with a low forehead, high cheekbones, protruding jaws, and a small chin. While the numerous nations that make up this race exhibit a unique range of intellectual character, with the lowest grade of humanity at the far extreme, the Negro is cheerful, adaptable, and sluggish...

Varied African countries have quite different moral and intellectual traditions. The negroes are known to enjoy their pastimes and engage in them with great vigor. For them, a day of work is no barrier to a night of fun.

Like the majority of other barbaric nations, their institutions usually exhibit violence and superstition. They seem to like fighting and possess a fair amount of fortitude on a personal level, but once defeated, they submit to fate and adjust to changing conditions with astonishing ease.

The Negroes lack originality but have high imitation skills, allowing them to quickly pick up mechanics. They have extraordinary musical talent, and all of their senses are incredibly keen.

Chapter 4

Decline in Empire

When attempting to predict where the United States is headed, there are compelling reasons to turn to Rome rather than any other civilization. Rome's decline is well known, yet few people can explain why. Even fewer, in my opinion, are aware that the United States is currently moving in the same direction for many of the same reasons, which I'll discuss in a moment.

Around the year 107, when Trajan completed the conquest of Dacia, Rome attained its military zenith (the territory of modern Romania). The empire's size peaked with Dacia, but on nearly all other metrics, I'd argue it had already passed its apex.

In some senses, the U.S. attained its absolute peak in the 1950s, as well as its peak relative to the rest of the world. This nation produced 80% of the world's cars and 50% of its GNP in 1950. It now accounts for 5% of global cars and nearly 21% of global GNP. One-fourth of the world's gold reserves are presently held by it, down from two-thirds. It was by far the largest creditor in the world, but it is now by far the largest debtor. The average

American's income used to be by far the highest in the world; it now ranks somewhere around sixth and is declining.

But Western culture as a whole, not just in the United States, is in decline. Politically, economically, and militarily, Europe dominated practically the whole world in 1910. It is now evolving into a Chinese Disneyland complete with genuine buildings and a petting zoo. Compared to the US, it has fallen much more.

Rome, like America, was established by immigrants, supposedly from Troy. In its early years, it had monarchs as its leaders, just like America. Later, the Romans established a Senate, and many Assemblies, and became autonomous. Power eventually shifted to the executive, which was most likely no coincidence.

The architecture of government buildings, the choice of the eagle as the national bird, the employment of Latin mottos, and the inappropriate usage of the fasces—the axe surrounded by rods—as a symbol of state power are all examples of how the founders of the United States modeled their nation after Rome. The Federalist Papers' pseudonymous author, Publius, derived his name from one of

Rome's first consuls. Military prowess is vital to American identity, just as it was in ancient Rome. When you seriously follow a model, you start to resemble it.

Since Edward Gibbon's publication of The Decline and Fall of the Roman Empire in 1776—the same year that Adam Smith's Wealth of Nations and the U.S. Declaration of Independence were written—a sizable cottage industry has sprung up comparing ancient and contemporary eras. I love all three a lot, but D&F stands out for me since it's not just a fantastic history but also a work of art. And it's hilarious; Gibbon had a deft sense of humor.

Since Gibbon's day, significant strides have been made in our comprehension of Rome thanks to archeological findings. Because he was as much a philologist as a historian and based his writing on what the ancients claimed about themselves, there were many things he just didn't know.

When Gibbon wrote, there was no genuine science of archeology; little had even been done to correlate what was on the surviving monuments, even the well-known monuments, and on the coins, with what was on the remaining ancient manuscripts. Not to mention archaeologists searched the provinces for what remained of Roman villas, battlefields, and other such structures. Gibbon, like the majority of historians, thus tended to gather hearsay.

And how could he decide which of the historical sources to trust? It's as if George Carlin, Gore Vidal, H. L. Mencken, Norman Mailer, and William F. Buckley all published different accounts of the same incident, and you had to decide which one was accurate. That would make it difficult to determine what transpired just a few years ago, let alone in the distant past. Because so much of history is "he said/she said," it is very tendentious.

In any case, perhaps you don't want a history lesson from the distant past. Some educated suggestions about what the United States is most likely to experience would likely amuse you more. I have some.

The fall of Rome may not have been a positive thing, in my opinion. As with most civilizations, Rome had a lot of excellent qualities. However, there were many other aspects of Rome that I found objectionable, including its anti-commercialism, militarism, and, after Caesar, its increasingly centralized and dictatorial government. In light of this, it is worthwhile to question whether the fall of the United States could not be a positive thing.

Then why did Rome crumble? Demandt, a German, compiled 210 justifications in 1985. Some of them, including racial degradation, homosexuality, and excessive freedom, strikes me as ridiculous. Most are unnecessary. Some are simply common sense, such as insolvency, moral decline, and corruption.

The list by Gibbon is substantially shorter. He attributed the fall of Rome to just two factors, one internal and one external: Christianity and barbarian invasions, respectively. However, it's rather difficult, to sum up, his six big volumes in one line. I believe Gibbon was fundamentally correct in both cases. However, he looked at early Christianity (that is, from its founding to the middle of the fourth century) extremely lightly due to the sensibilities of his day; I've chosen to deal with it less delicately. Hopefully, not too many readers will be disturbed by my interpretation of religion or barbarian invasions (both then and now).

In any case, accepting Gibbon's fundamental assumptions about Christians and barbarians, I decided to further categorize the factors contributing to Rome's decline into ten groups, which I will now discuss: political, legal, social, demographic, ecological, military, psychological, intellectual, religious, and economic. And as a bonus, I'll offer you one more, totally unrelated, and crucial explanation for why both Rome and the U.S. fell apart near the end of this essay.

You don't have to agree with my interpretation, but let's look at the lessons Rome's history can teach us, from its semi-mythical founding by Romulus and Remus in 753 BCE (a story that conflicts with Virgil's account of Aeneas and the refugee Trojans) to what is typically considered to be the end of the Western empire in 476 AD when the child-emperor Romulus Augustulus was overthrown by Odoacer (an It resembles the recent two hundred years of American history quite a bit. Conquest and expansion came first, followed by worldwide supremacy and fall.

Political
Speaking of Rome's easy demise is somewhat deceptive; it is much more realistic to speak of its slow transition, punctuated by periods of what paleontologists refer to as "punctuated disequilibrium." There were a lot of slips.

Republican With the ascension of Augustus and the beginning of the so-called Principate, Rome was destroyed in 31 BCE. It nearly fell apart in the 50 years of the middle of the third century, a time of ongoing civil conflict, the beginning of significant barbarian incursions, and the demise of the denarius, Rome's silver coin.

In the 290s, Rome's status as a free society began to decline. Later, under Diocletian and throughout the Dominate era, the city underwent another major upheaval (more on this shortly). The Goths' destruction of a Roman army at Adrianople in 378 and the start of widespread invasions may have signaled the end. When Alaric, a Goth who was a Roman general, led the first sacking of Rome, perhaps we could declare 410 to be the end.

One could argue that the civilization didn't truly fall apart until the late 600s when Islam seized control of the Middle East and North Africa and shut down trade with the Mediterranean. Perhaps we ought to use 1453, the year of the fall of Constantinople and the Eastern Empire. The Pope is the Pontifex Maximus and wears red shoes, just like Julius Caesar did when he was in that position, so perhaps the Empire is still with us now in the form of the Catholic Church.

The Principate period marks the beginning of Rome's rapid trend toward absolutism, centralization, totalitarianism, and bureaucracy, which is one certain reflection in the faraway mirror. I believe we can agree that Roosevelt's election in 1933 marked the beginning of the American Principate, during which the president similarly ruled over Congress to how Augustus ruled over the Senate. The use of pretenses decreased with time in Rome, just as it has in the United States.

The Principate period—during which the emperor, at least in theory, was only the first among equals—was replaced after the third century by the Dominate period, during which the emperor became an absolute monarch as a result of ongoing civil conflict and currency collapse. Diocletian rose to power in 284 and Constantine followed in 306 following another civil war. From that moment on, the emperor was regarded as an eastern potentate and never even pretended to be the foremost among equals. However, it must be emphasized that the president is now guarded by hundreds or perhaps thousands of bodyguards, indicating that the same trend is in action in the U.S. The last president to venture outside and casually stroll through DC like a regular citizen while in office was Harry Truman.

The American people are plagued by a phantom: the specter of decline. As the winning presidential candidate used the slogan "Make America Great Again," which meant that America was no longer as great as it once was, discussion of decline jumped from academic treatises to the forefront of public discourse in 2016. Trump's agenda was based on the idea that America needs to take extreme measures to reverse a decline brought on by its government. The 2008 financial crisis, the government's response to it, and the absolute decrease in income and well-being for a growing segment of Americans all served to highlight the magnitude of economic and political inequality in the United States.

For those of us living in America in the early twenty-first century, signs of decline are obvious. Even though bridges are collapsing, water and sewer lines are bursting, dams are failing, air and road traffic is getting worse, and passenger trains are struggling to run at speeds comparable to those of the early 20th century, spending on infrastructure has remained static.

A vacation to most of Europe and East Asia can look to an American like travel to a Tomorrowland, never to be realized in the United States outside of Disney World, from the airport arrival through the high-speed train or subway excursion into town.

The highest levels of student achievement at the primary, secondary, and collegiate levels have declined. Students in the US perform worse than their classmates in nations with far lower levels of affluence or educational spending because they attend schools that are getting worse and worse. The United States, which led the developed world in the percentage of its people with university degrees for the next five decades after inventing mass higher education with the GI Bill in 1944, has now slipped to fifteenth place.

The military and the healthcare system are two areas where the United States does spend extensively, yet its relative performance in both areas has been declining for decades. The life expectancy of countries is currently ranked by the

United States at number 34. According to Beckfield and Morris,

In comparison to those living in any other wealthy democracy, Americans today may anticipate having shorter and sicker lives. This "health gap" between the US and its peer nations is widening over time as the death rates for those between the ages of 45 and 54 continue to decline in Canada, the UK, Australia, France, Germany, and Sweden while remaining stable in the US. The prevalence of poor health is comparable to the former Soviet-bloc states of Central and Eastern Europe, and the level of [health] disparity in the US is significantly higher than that seen in the majority of European nations.

This is true even though US medical spending in 2013 accounted for 17.1% of GDP, about 50% higher than France, which ranked second with 11.6 percent. In 2013, the United States paid $9,086 per person, which was 44 percent more than Switzerland, which came in second with $6,325.

Why do Americans receive such a poor return on their health care investments? Or, to put it another way, why does it cost so much to provide care that is inferior to that which is offered in other wealthy and less fortunate nations? It's not because Americans use so much healthcare, compared to people in other OECD nations, Americans visit the doctor less frequently and stay in the hospital for fewer days.

Due to its recurrent failure to accomplish military goals over decades, America stands out among the world's dominating nations over the previous 500 years.
Instead, because Congress has repeatedly rejected cost restraints and prevents the federal government from negotiating costs, Americans spend significantly more than anybody else on Earth for doctors, pharmaceuticals, medical devices, and hospital stays. Additionally, compared to other OECD countries, America spends more than twice as much on administrative expenditures for healthcare.

This is because numerous for-profit insurance companies, each with their own set of procedures and reimbursement schedules, must hire armies of administrators to process their unique forms, while hospitals and doctors' offices employ medical "coders" who aim to classify the care provided to patients in ways that maximize reimbursements. As a result, insurance companies are forced to hire even more administrators to check and challenge the bills submitted by hospitals and physicians. Naturally, none of that has any bearing on the well-being or longevity of patients.

Even as its expenditure advantage and the quantity and sophistication of its armaments over its real and potential enemies have increased to a level unheard of in world history, the US military has grown ever less capable of winning wars. The first Gulf War in 1991, which had the only aim of driving Iraq out of Kuwait, and various "police actions" against pitifully minor and helpless foes in the Dominican Republic in 1965, Grenada in 1983, and Panama in 1989 are the only clear-cut American military wins since World War II.

While the US war in Vietnam was a definite loss, the one in Korea had an unclear outcome. The United States fought against sizable foes supported by the opposing superpower in both of those wars, and in Korea, it also faced off against tens of thousands of Chinese forces. None of those circumstances apply to the wars in Iraq and Afghanistan, which, while they did not result in an absolute victory, failed to accomplish the majority of their goals.

Any single setback can be explained by specific, unforeseen circumstances, but America stands out among the world's superpowers over the previous 500 years for repeatedly failing to accomplish military goals over a long period. The fact that those failures took place in the absence of a military opponent on the rise and while America's capacity and willingness to produce and pay for the weapons required for military supremacy remained unaffected makes them all the more extraordinary.

The prognosis is gloomy outside of the lavishly if ineffectively, funded military and medical sectors. The ability of the federal, state, and municipal governments to raise the money is deteriorating just as more investment is required for infrastructure, scientific and industrial research and development, education, and environmental rehabilitation.

Federal revenue decreased in 2004 to 16.3% of GDP, the lowest level since 1951, as a result of the Bush tax cuts. Since 2000, governmental debt has significantly expanded, mirroring how American families have used credit to maintain their spending in the face of stagnating salaries. This has been done to maintain expenditure as tax revenues have decreased. From 31.7 percent in 1981 to 67.7

percent in 2008, the federal debt as a percentage of GDP more than doubled. Following the Great Recession, the federal debt as a percentage of GDP further rose to 101.8 percent in 2015.

In those three decades, private debt held by people and businesses grew as a percentage of GDP at an even higher rate, reaching four times the level of federal debt just before the financial crisis. "Between 2000 and 2007—the total [of household debt] doubled to $14 trillion and the household debt-to-income ratio exploded from 1.4 to 2.1," the report states. However, financial institutions' debt increased at the greatest rate, from 19.7% of GDP in 1979 to 117.9% of GDP in 2007.

Many analysts have discussed America's downfall and offered numerous solutions. There have been many recommendations for measures that could halt the decline of America's position as the world's leading economy and military power, as well as its inhabitants' ongoing decline from the top spot in terms of health, education, and well-being. However, those proposals are increasingly made with the resignation that they will not be taken seriously because the United States is no longer able to muster the political will necessary to appropriate the necessary funds and has lost the organizational ability to complete large-scale projects. Progressives and realists in America essentially convey their political choices as a sequence of regrets:

We all agree that the country with the strongest economy in the twenty-first century will develop a green energy sector. However, because America lacks China's riches and the EU's willingness to tax and regulate, this sector cannot genuinely thrive in this country.

We are aware that the best—possibly the only—way to reduce medical expenses and improve patient outcomes is through a government-run and financed universal health care system, but because of the insurance, pharmaceutical, and hospital sectors, this will never be possible in the United States. As a result, Americans will continue to pay more for poorer patient outcomes.

Every country with better educational outcomes has a single national system that rewards teachers' professionalism with high levels of autonomy and compensation, but America has a history of local control and, in any case, we can't afford to pay enough to hire capable professionals, so we had better settle for closely monitoring teachers by testing their students on fundamental academic skills, even though students who pass those tests are not prepared for higher education or in the workforce.

Commentators engage in magical thinking, expecting a savior or the unplanned eruption of a social movement when they do not despair about the effects of a purportedly singular American approach to politics and administration. In 2008, Barack Obama most clearly represented these ambitions, as his supporters looked to him for personal traits that would enable him to successfully bridge partisan differences and implement important reforms. "We are the folks we have been waiting for," Obama told the crowds during his rallies in return.

The extent to which progressive plans are founded on expectations of elite generosity rather than practical strategies for political mobilization is demonstrated by Ralph Nader's utopian novel Only the Super-Rich Can Save Us!, which imagines billionaires challenging corporate power and reviving citizen action. The fact that this book was published by the American who has been the most effective at creating citizen organizations over the past 50 years is particularly instructive and disturbing.

In any case, spending from the Koch brothers and their allies for federal and state-level candidates committed to eliminating environmental protections, weakening unions, and making it difficult for African Americans and other Democrats to win elections overwhelmed contributions from liberal billionaires like Tom Steyer, a hedge fund manager who spent tens of millions of dollars on advertisements criticizing Republican climate change skeptics in the 2014 and 2016 elections with little success.

Adherents of the "Tea Party" thought that by electing a group of retired corporate executives, contented heirs, career politicians, and various oddballs, they could drastically cut government spending, boost the economy, and restore politics to the way they believed the Founding Fathers intended it to be.

A fresh third party is periodically viewed as the force behind change. Ralph Nader believed that his third-party presidential run would upend the two-party oligopoly on power and, in some unspecified fashion, provide a space for progressive politics before he put his hopes in the hands of the superrich. The most well-known US newspaper columnist of the early twenty-first century, Thomas Friedman, called for a third candidate to address the American people directly during the upcoming presidential debate, saying, "These two parties are lying to you. They are both constrained by long-standing special interests, so they are unable to tell you the truth. I won't give you the information you want to hear. If we want to lead the globe and not become the new Romans, I'm going to tell you what you need to hear.

Even once political obstacles are overcome and a new program is put into place, implementation is hampered by the state's limited organizational capabilities.
It is unclear from Friedman's explanation how such a party might operate or raise money without acknowledging the "special interests" that support the two established parties. He also doesn't address how or why a third party would be able to get past the challenges that Obama, who also vowed to tell the truth, take on special interests, and break through gridlock, was unable to do.

Even though they work within the Republican Party, Tea Party activists think that a new, more pure party may revive the country in (unspecified) ways that even a purified and reenergized Republican Party cannot.

Another well-known cliché suggests that new technologies have the potential to revolutionize politics. It has yet to be proven if effective political movements that can displace failing or shrinking unions and mass organizations can be fostered by the internet, Twitter, or cell phones. The fact that Donald Trump uses Twitter does not indicate that it can be used as a tool for organizing. Because journalists are "a group as intoxicated by Twitter as Mr. Trump is," Twitter worked for Trump. As a result, each of his tweets was amplified by traditional broadcast media, ensuring that "the social media platforms that had been hailed as democratic tools could also be used to undermine democratic norms."

As with the previous technological advancement, direct mail, which was invented during George McGovern's 1972 presidential campaign, the internet has proven to be the most successful fundraising tool so far. However, money collected in a 19th-century way, from corporations and wealthy individuals who buy the votes of candidates and officials of both parties, continues to outpace money raised online or through the mail.

Even once political obstacles are overcome and a new program is put into place, implementation is hampered by the state's limited organizational capabilities. Compare President Obama's 2010 health care legislation to Medicare, which began operating with 19 million individuals covered just 11 months after Lyndon Johnson signed it into law in 1965. A four-year transition period was built into the recent law before its government-supervised health care plans went into effect.

This protracted delay was partially an attempt to circumvent the CBO's accounting guidelines, but it also reflected the consensus of the president and Congress that the government could not put such a plan into action any faster. When the Obama administration delayed the implementation of some parts of the law from 2014 to 2015 and the online system to register applicants for government-subsidized insurance failed to function properly for several months, that belief proved to be more than justified.

Alternatively, contrast the 2009 stimulus with the New Deal's government employment initiatives or the 2009 stimulus spending in China. The "shovel-ready" projects carried out in the US in 2009–10 were small-scale and incremental, with a primary focus on repaving roads and repairing existing infrastructure, paying for current state and local workers who would have been laid off and dispersing tax breaks to be spent on consumer goods in the private sector. This was due to the lack of agencies capable of preparing engineering or architectural plans and managing a corps of newly hired workers.

Overall, the stimulus spending had little to no impact on building the new utility, transportation, and other networks required for international competitiveness or even to maintain current levels of economic production. Instead, it merely slowed the rapid deterioration of American roads, bridges, dams, and schools. The US government's ability to plan and carry out significant projects is declining, coinciding with the loss of its capacity to administer benefits, as evidenced by the contrast between the massive dams and other projects built during the New Deal and the high-speed rail lines, subways, airports, and city centers accelerated by the Chinese stimulus.
TOP

Chapter 5

Constitutional War

Japan and World War II

Congress has only declared war eleven times in the history of the United States, but taking a closer look at one of these declarations will illustrate how the process works.On December 7, 1941, the Japanese military attacked Pearl Harbor, a U.S. naval base in Hawaii, and destroyed much of the United States' Pacific fleet.The next morning, President Franklin D. Roosevelt approached Congress and formally requested that the United States go to war.

President Roosevelt told members of Congress that the unprovoked attack by Japan served as justification for committing the United States to join World War II. Furthermore, he asked that Congress authorize his use and control of the United States' military forces.In this situation, Congress immediately pulled all pending legislation related to Japan, considered President Roosevelt's declaration as a joint resolution, and suspended some procedural rules that would slow down the approval process. It took less than a day for Congress to declare war. The joint resolution passed the House of Representatives and Senate nearly unanimously.

What Happens Afterwards

Once a declaration of war has been approved by Congress, a "state of war" under international law becomes effective. This means that the United States may commence "the killing of enemy combatants, the seizure of enemy property, and the apprehension of enemy aliens." Additionally, the declaration of war terminates all diplomatic and commercial relations between the United States and its adversary and suspends most treaties that the two have signed.An official declaration of war has ramifications in the domestic sphere as well. When Congress declares war, many "standby statutes" are automatically activated, conferring special powers onto the President. These powers can have drastic consequences. For example, under one statute, the President can order manufacturing plants to produce armaments for the military. If the manufacturing plants refuse to do so, the President can order the military to seize the plants. Another statute allows the President and executive agencies to conduct electronic surveillance without a court order for some time after Congress declares war.

A formal declaration of war also activates the Alien Enemy Act, allowing the President to apprehend, restrain, secure, and remove all natives from, or citizens of, the hostile nation from the United States, unless these people have been naturalized.For example, during World War I, President Woodrow Wilson used the powers conferred by this Act to prevent German aliens from possessing firearms or explosives.

Congress' Role During War

In addition to Congress' ability to declare a war, it also has the power to oversee it and most importantly, determine how and whether it is funded.First, Congress, not the executive branch, has "the power of the purse" over the military. Article I, Section 8 says that Congress has the power "To raise and support Armies."If Congress decides that it does not want to allocate a budget to military matters, such as the manufacture of additional weapons or the raising of more soldiers, it can decline to do so.Thus, Congress can place financial hurdles in front of the President and make a war extremely difficult for him to wage.

Congress can also affect the United States' status in a war by declaring war on some enemies while declining to do so in the case of others. For example, in World War II, the United States declared war on Germany, Italy, Japan, Bulgaria, Hungary and Romania, but not on Axis participant Finland.Congress can define the nature of war by limiting the scope of a declaration of war, though this has never actually been done.Finally, Congress can declare an end to a war by passing legislation that cancels the existing state of war.Like any other piece of legislation, however, this can be vetoed by the president (though as always, the veto can be overridden by a two-thirds majority of Congress).

Unilateral Presidential Actions

So, if the United States has not declared war since 1942, how is it that we been involved in so many military actions since? The answer is that as commander-in-chief of the military, the president can simply order the military about without a declaration of war, and virtually every president has taken advantage of this ability. Though Congress has stopped short of declaring war, Congress has given the president express authority to conduct military actions several times since World War II, including the Gulf of Tonkin Resolution in 1964[20] that led to the Vietnam "War" and Authorization for Use of Military Force in 2001 while led to military actions in Afghanistan. After the Vietnam War,

Congress did pass the War Powers Resolution of 1973, which limited the President's power to engage in foreign military actions without congressional consent.However, the enforceability of this resolution is unclear.As a practical matter, no Presidential military action has been successfully challenged under the War Powers Resolution.

While the declaration of war may be a thing of the past in United States diplomacy, Congress retains means to affect the President's ability to conduct military actions. As such, the constitutional split of military powers between the president and Congress remains very much in effect.